Geography Starts

CAVES

Claire Llewellyn

Heinemann Library
Chicago, Illinois

Customer Service 888-454-2279

Visit our website at www.heinemannlibrary.com

Designed by David Oakley
Illustrations by Hardlines (p. 13) and Jo Brooker
Printed and bound in China by South China Printing Company.
06
10 9 8 7 6

Library of Congress Cataloging-in-Publication Data
Llewellyn, Claire.
 Caves / Claire Llewellyn.
  p. cm. – (Geography starts)
 Includes bibliographical references (p.) and index.
 Summary: Describes the geologic conditions that lead to the formation of both sea
caves and underground caves and presents unusual rock formations and animal life found
in caves.
  ISBN 1-57572-202-X (lib. bdg.) ISBN 1-58810-968-2 (pbk. bdg.)
 1. Caves—Juvenile literature. [1. Caves.] I. Title. II. Series.
GB601.2.L554 2000
551.44'7—dc21
                 99-053329

Acknowledgments
The Publishers would like to thank the following for permission to reproduce photographs:
Bruce Coleman, p. 29; Ecoscene/Rob Nichol, p. 9; Ecoscene/Sally Morgan, p. 12; FLPA/John Bastable, p. 8; FLPA/W.
Wisniewski, p. 10; FLPA/Terry Whittaker, p. 11; FLPA/Chris Demetriou, p. 17; NRSC/Airphoto Group/Forestry
Commission, pp. 22, 24; Oxford Scientific Films/Alastair Shay, p. 4; Oxford Scientific Films/Kim Westerskov, p .6; Martyn
Chillmaid, p. 7; Oxford Scientific Films/Mills Tandy, p. 14; Oxford Scientific Films/JAL Cooke, p. 19; Oxford Scientific
Films/T. Middleton, p. 20; Robert Harding Picture Library/A. C. Waltham, p.15; Robert Harding Picture Library/MPH, p.
16; Robert Harding Picture Library/Richard Ashworth, p. 28; Still Pictures/D. Escartin, p. 18; Telegraph Color
Library/Masterfile, p. 5, Telegraph Color Library/Jean Marc Blache, p. 21; White Scar Caves, p. 26.

Cover photograph reproduced with permission of Robert Harding Picture Library.

Some words are shown in bold, **like this**. You can find
out what they mean by looking in the glossary.

Contents

What Is a Cave?

A cave is a hollow space under the ground or in a hillside. Caves are formed when rock is worn away over time.

This cave has been made under the ground.

This cave has been made under the sea.

There are caves all over the world. They are found along the **coast,** deep in the ground, and in the sides of mountains and hills.

Making Sea Caves

The sea is very powerful. All along the **coast,** strong waves batter the cliffs. Over many years, the sea wears away the rock.

Day after day, the sea crashes against the foot of the cliff.

The foot of this cliff has been worn away.

The moving water eats into the bottom of the cliff. If there is a weak part in the rock, the sea can start to make a hole in the bottom of the cliff.

How Sea Caves Grow

The sea has made caves in these rocky cliffs.

In some places, the bottom of a cliff begins to crack. The cracks are made bigger and bigger by the sea. Slowly, the cracks are made into caves.

Sea water shoots up through a blowhole in the roof of a cave.

Some sea caves have cracks in the roof. As the sea water pushes against the cracks, it makes a hole called a **blowhole.**

Making an Arch

Sometimes two sea caves meet back-to-back. As the rock between them is worn away, it forms an **arch** in the rock.

This arch used to be two separate sea caves.

These pillars of rock are on the **coast** of Australia.

Over many years, the roof of the arch is worn away, too. It falls down into the sea. This leaves a **pillar** of rock standing up in the sea. The pillar is called a **stack**.

Underground Caves

Caves are sometimes found underground. They are almost always found in places where the rock is made of **limestone**.

These hills are made of limestone. Caves have formed inside them.

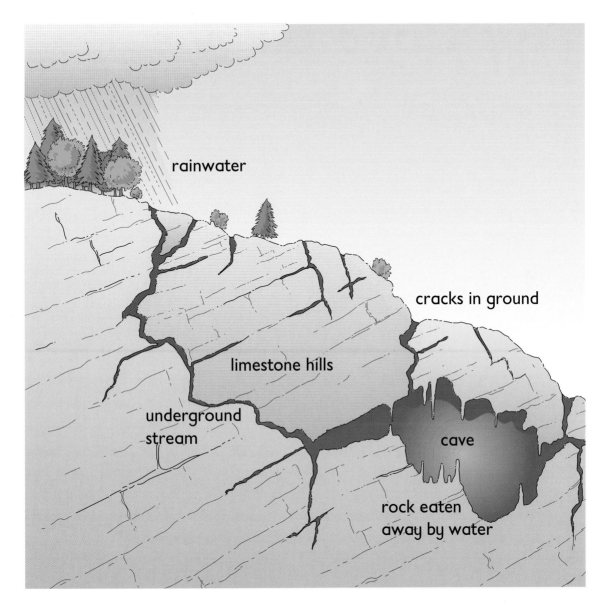

rainwater

cracks in ground

limestone hills

underground stream

cave

rock eaten away by water

Rainwater can **dissolve** the limestone. The water trickles down through cracks in the ground. It slowly wears away the rocks below. After a long time, a cave is made.

The Cave Grows

This huge cave has been made by water flowing underground.

It can take thousands of years for underground streams to **dissolve** the **limestone**. Cracks in the rock grow bigger and bigger until they make huge tunnels and caves.

The only way to visit this cave is in a boat!

Some underground caves and tunnels are flooded with water. Others are dry.

In the Cave

Strange rock shapes can grow in some caves.

The drops of water that trickle underground contain tiny pieces of **limestone**. Some of the drops dry up as they fall, leaving the tiny rock pieces behind. These pile up inside caves.

Fingers of rock hang from the roof of a cave. They are called **stalactites**. **Pillars** of rock grow up from the floor of a cave. They are called **stalagmites**.

Stalactites and stalagmites are formed very slowly over thousands of years.

Hill Caves

People made these drawings in a cave in **Algeria** thousands of years ago.

Some caves are in the sides of mountains and hills. Wind, wet weather, and running water wore away the rock. Caves have been used for shelter for thousands of years.

In some places, shepherds still use caves to shelter their sheep. Many wild animals, such as bats, use caves for shelter, too.

These bats rest in caves by day and go out to feed at night.

Exploring Caves

People who study caves are called **speleologists**. They study the rocks and draw maps of the tunnels and caves.

These speleologists are studying an underground tunnel.

These men are wearing **protective** clothing in this flooded tunnel.

Exploring caves can be dangerous because they are sometimes flooded when it rains. To be safe, speleologists often take diving gear and boats.

Cave Map 1

This photo was taken by an airplane. You can see high **limestone** hills. Between the hills, you can see a river and a road. You can also see two **quarries** by the road.

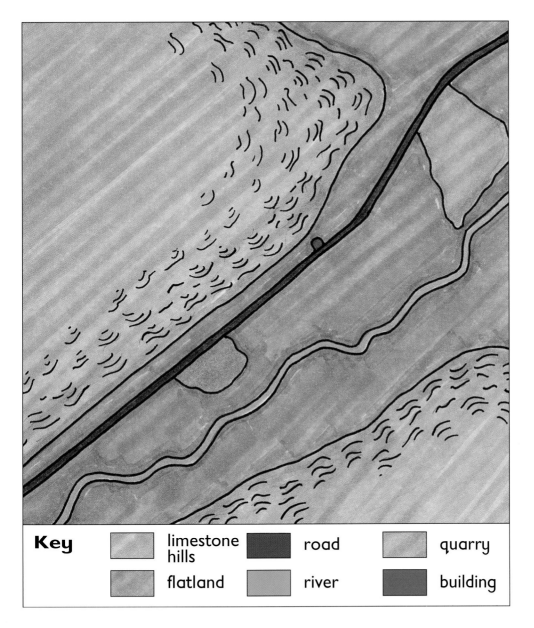

Key   limestone hills   road   quarry

flatland   river   building

Maps are pictures of the land. This map shows us the same place as the photo. The key tells us what each color means. The brown color shows the hills. The green color shows the flatland.

Cave Map 2

This photo shows a smaller part of the land, but you can see it more clearly. You can see some buildings along the road. One of the buildings is the entrance to some caves that are under the hills.

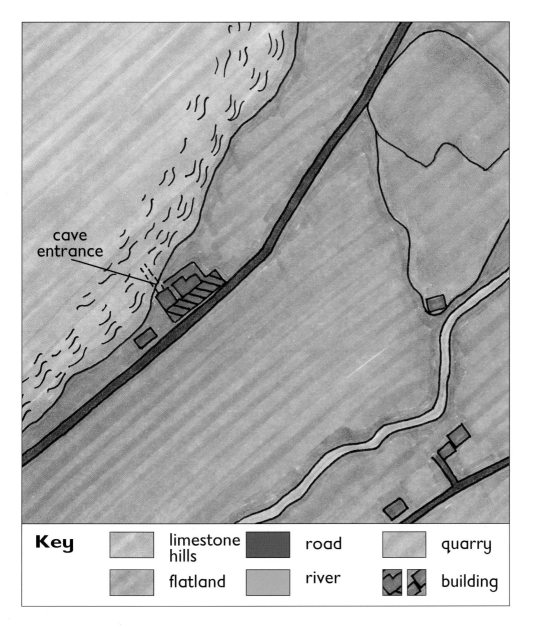

cave entrance

Key

	limestone hills		road		quarry
	flatland		river		building

Maps give people useful information. This map shows how to get to the caves. It shows the buildings at the entrance of the caves in red. The black stripes show visitors where to park their cars.

Cave Map 3

This photo shows one of the underground caves. It is called Battlefield Cavern. The cave has many **stalactites**. People must go through an underground tunnel to reach the cave.

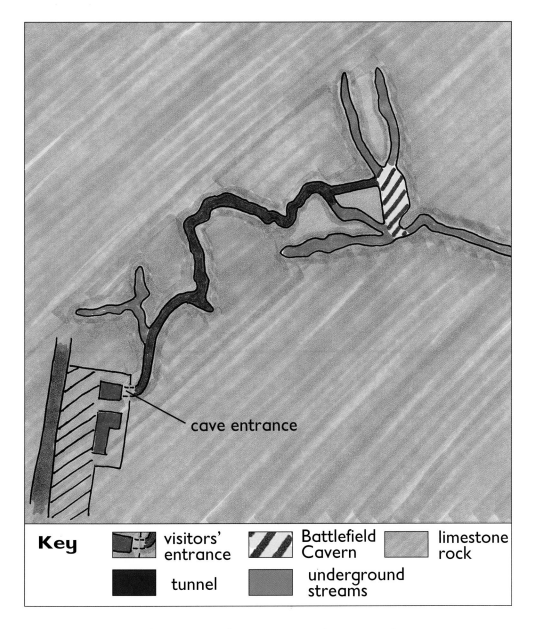

cave entrance

Key

visitors' entrance	Battlefield Cavern	limestone rock
tunnel	underground streams	

This map shows the way from the cave entrance to Battlefield Cavern. The purple color shows the underground tunnel. Some parts of the tunnel have streams in them. The rocks around the cave are colored brown.

Amazing Cave Facts

The world's largest cave **chamber** is the Sarawak Chamber in Malaysia. It would have room for about 40 football fields inside it!

Mammoth Cave **National Park** in Kentucky contains caves that stretch for a long way. Laid end-to-end, they would reach from Cleveland, Ohio to Washington, D.C.

Glossary

Algeria   country in Africa, a large area of land that is south of Europe

arch   curved rock on top of two tall stacks of rock

blowhole   hole in the roof of a cave that water from the ocean rushes through

chamber   space like a room inside a cave

coast   land that is at the edge of the ocean

dissolve   to disappear in water

limestone   kind of rock that is easily cut and shaped

national park   land that is set aside by law to keep it safe and beautiful

pillar   thin, tall pile of rock

protective   keeps people safe

quarry   place where sand or stone is dug out of the ground

speleologist   person who studies caves (You say spee-lee-AH-lo-jist.)

stack   pile of rock left standing in the ocean when the curved part on top has fallen down

stalactite   finger of rock that grows down from the roof of a cave

stalagmite   pillar of rock that grows up from the floor of a cave

More Books to Read

Armentrout, Patricia. *Caves*. Vero Beach, Fla.: Rourke Press, Inc., 1996.

Morris, Neil. *Caves*. Austin, Tex.: Raintree Steck-Vaughn Publishers, 1997.

Rigby, Susan. *Caves*. Mahwah, N.J.:Troll Communications, 1997.
An older reader can help you with this book.

Siebert, Diane. *Cave*. New York: Morrow, William & Company, Inc., 2000.

Index